love, Karyn

Christmas
1990

The
Naming of
Flowers

The Naming of Flowers

Anne Halpin

Illustrations by
Rob Proctor

HARPER & ROW, PUBLISHERS

NEW YORK

CAMBRIDGE, PHILADELPHIA, SAN FRANCISCO
LONDON, MEXICO CITY, SÃO PAULO, SYDNEY

THE NAMING OF FLOWERS was conceived and produced by
Running Heads Incorporated
55 West 21 Street
New York, N.Y. 10010

Senior Editor: Sarah Kirshner
Designer: Jan Melchior
Managing Editor: Lindsey Crittenden
Production Manager: Linda Winters

Library of Congress Catalog Card Number: 89-46533
Library of Congress Cataloging-in-Publication is available on this title.
ISBN: 0-06-016476-X

Typeset by Trufont Typographers
Color separations by Hong Kong Scanner Craft Co., Ltd.
Printed and bound in Singapore by Times Offset Pte Ltd.

10 9 8 7 6 5 4 3 2 1

ACKNOWLEDGMENTS

Thanks to John Michel at Harper & Row for his enthusiasm
and support for this book since the very beginning; and to
Marta Hallett, Sarah Kirshner, and the other people at Running Heads who worked on this book. Rob Proctor's gorgeous
art and Jan Melchior's lovely design speak for themselves.
Thanks are also due to Doug Smith for his help with Greek
and Latin etymology.

CONTENTS

INTRODUCTION

M ost of us become intrigued by plant names at one time or another. How can we help but wonder where a name like foxglove came from, or what a word such as *Geranium* means? Plant names are charming, amusing, sometimes perplexing, and often highly descriptive. The name "bellflower," for instance, nicely describes the form of *Campanula* blossoms; daylily flowers do indeed last only a single day.

Plants are known by different names in different countries, and a single plant may have many different names even in one country, or one neighborhood. Consider, for example, *Hesperis matronalis*. It is known as mother of the evening, dame's rocket, sweet rocket, and dame's violet, among other things. A way to sort out the confusion of vernacular plant names was devised in the eighteenth century by a Swedish botanist named Karl von Linné (Latinized after his death to Carolus Linnaeus). He worked out a system of botanical nomenclature that remains the basis of the system we use today. Like other scientific languages, Linné's system of nomenclature is in Latin, although many of the names have their roots in Greek.

By assigning to each plant its own unique botanical name, Linnaeus brought order to the chaos of plant naming. He gave each plant two names: the first is its genus, the second is its species. The generic, or genus, name tells us the plant's immediate grouping; *Aquilegia*, for example, identifies columbines. The second, or species, name identifies a particular plant within the genus; *Aquilegia caerulea* is the blue columbine.

Botanical names, like common names, come from any number of sources. They may have mythological origins, like *Achillea* or *Narcissus*. They may explain something about the appearance of a part of the plant, like *Dicentra* ("two spurs") or *Delphinium* ("dolphin"-shaped). Or they may have to do with the plant's behavior, like *Gypsophila* ("gypsum-loving"). Sometimes plant names commemorate eminent people in the field. In any case, becoming familiar with the Latin terminology can tell us something about a plant we may never have grown or even seen. When you see the word *erecta* in a plant name, you know that the plant has an upright growth habit. Conversely, *repens* indicates a plant that creeps.

This little book explains both the botanical and common names of twenty-seven popular garden flowers, and offers related snippets of the folklore and tradition surrounding them. Meander through its pages and you may come to know some of your favorite flowers more intimately.

ASTER

Aster

It is said that many years ago, when gods and goddesses roamed the heavens, the aster first appeared on earth. According to one legend, Asteria, Greek goddess of stars, looked down from Olympus upon the earth and was sad that she saw no stars there. The sight made her cry, and wherever her tears fell to the ground asters bloomed. According to another tale, Virgo sprinkled stardust over the earth and asters sprang up everywhere the stardust had landed. The goddesses must have scattered their dust and teardrops far and wide, for many species of asters are native to North America, and others to Europe and Asia.

Whatever their homeland, all asters are linked to the stars by their generic name. The flowers have been called starwort in England and Germany (the suffix "-wort" in a plant's name means that it once had medicinal uses), and asters have long been thought to possess magical healing powers. The ancient Greeks burned aster leaves to keep evil spirits away.

The two best-known garden species, the New England and New York asters, are both American natives introduced to Europe in 1637. English gardeners took the flowers to their hearts, giving both autumn-blooming species the collective name Michaelmas daisy, for St. Michael's Day, September 29.

BELLFLOWER
Campanula

Campanulas are known by many names, but "bellflower" most aptly describes the shape of the nodding violet or white blossoms. The generic name comes from *campana*, which means "bell" in Latin. You may also find various species of *Campanula* referred to as Canterbury bells, wild hyacinth, harebell, Our Lady's nightcap (or thimble), coventry bells, or chimney bellflower.

The epithet with the most interesting story attached is Venus' looking glass. Venus, goddess of beauty, had a magic mirror that reflected back nothing but beauty to anyone who looked into it. One day Venus lost her mirror, and it was found by a shepherd boy. The poor lad became so fascinated with the magic glass that he could not give it up. Venus sent Cupid to retrieve her mirror, but in his hurry to get it back he knocked it out of the boy's hand. The mirror shattered, and everywhere a piece landed the namesake flower grew.

The names of various *Campanula* species describe the flowers, the plants, or their place of origin. One interestingly titled species is *Campanula pyramidalis*, the chimney bellflower. Its name has been related to an old practice of growing the plants in pots and using them to fill unused fireplaces during the summer.

BLEEDING HEART
Dicentra

🌿 Any child growing up where bleeding heart is planted has found herself (or himself) investigating the little heart-shaped flowers that dangle in rows from their slender horizontal stems. They look for all the world like strings of little lockets dancing in the breeze.

As far as the common name goes, the projecting white petals are supposed to represent drops of blood flowing from the heart. Curious observers who turn the heart upside down can also see in the narrow white petals the form of the

mysterious lady in the locket and thus understand the source of some more romantic names for the flowers, such as lady-in-the-bath and lady's locket.

The flowers consist of a flattened pair of pink outer petals, each of which has a spur at its base (these petals are the two halves of the heart), with narrow white inner petals projecting from between the halves. The plant's botanic name, from the Greek, describes the flower structure: *di* ("two") and *kentron* ("spur"). The species name of the bleeding heart, *spectabilis*, means "remarkable." But the flower's peculiar shape and spurs are really more quietly charming than remarkable, a gift to the imagination as well as the eye.

BUTTERFLY WEED

Asclepias

The most famous wild member of the genus *Asclepias* is the common milkweed, whose ripe pods open to release clouds of seeds that drift across fields and damp meadows on fluffy little parachutes, touching down to start new colonies of plants. But this genus of American natives also includes a popular garden flower, whose common name, butterfly weed, is a tipoff to its attraction for those gauzy-winged harlequins of summer. The bright orange flowers of butterfly weed are certain to lure some butterflies to your garden.

Although milkweed and butterfly weed are quite different in appearance, they share in common a thick, milky sap within their stems and leaves. This sap was once thought to have medicinal powers, although in truth it is poisonous. But it is in honor of its supposed healing virtues that the plant was dubbed *Asclepias*. The name commemorates Aesculapius, a son of Apollo who was raised by the centaur Chiron (see CORNFLOWER, p. 21, for his story). Chiron taught Aesculapius the art of healing, and the boy grew up to become a renowned physician. He was worshipped in Rome as the god of medicine.

Perhaps our butterfly weed cannot heal our physical ills, but the sight of the lovely butterflies it draws into our gardens is surely a tonic for the spirit.

COLUMBINE
Aquilegia

Waving and dancing in the breeze atop slender stems, columbines suggest birds in flight, and indeed, both the botanical and common names describe the resemblance of the flowers to birds. The botanical name, *Aquilegia*, comes from the Latin word for "eagle," *aquila*: the spurs on the petals suggest the claws of a mighty bird of prey. The plant's common name is taken from another Latin word, *columba*, which means "dove." The flowers were thought to resemble a group of pigeons or doves clustered together.

Though the dove symbolizes innocence and gentleness — a fitting allusion for such a graceful blossom — the Victorians assigned the columbine a meaning of thanklessness or folly in their flower language. It would seem the association derives from a seventeenth-century comparison of the pointed petals to horns, presumably the horns of a cuckolded husband. In some quarters the flower was imagined to look like a jester's cap and bells, hence the connection with foolishness.

In contrast to the rather colorful derivations of the columbine's common and generic names, most of the species names simply describe the flowers, the plants, or their habitat. *Aquilegia caerulea*, for example, is named for its deep blue flowers, while *A. canadensis* is native to North America. And *A. flabellata*, the fan columbine, has fan-shaped leaves.

CORNFLOWER
BACHELOR'S BUTTON
Centaurea

The common names for this plant are rather prosaic in origin. "Bachelor's button" comes from the flower's popularity as a boutonniere. The name "cornflower" originated in England, where the plant often grew wild in fields of grain.

The genus *Centaurea* takes its name from the Greek centaurs, a mythical race of beings who were half man and half horse, and renowned for their wisdom. Chief among the centaurs was Chiron, whose skills in hunting, medicine, music, and the art of prophecy were deeply respected. He served as tutor of many of the great heroes of Greek mythology. On one occasion Chiron was sorely wounded by a poisoned arrow, and after pulling it out he used the blossoms of a cornflower to heal his injury.

The species name of the cornflower, *cyanus*, is taken from the Greek *cyan*, meaning "blue." The name is said to commemorate Cyanus, a mythical flower-loving boy who spent all his time wandering through fields and meadows making garlands. The cornflower was his favorite and when he died he was found lying in a bed of them. Flora, the goddess of flowers, turned him into the heavenly blue flower in appreciation of his devotion.

CRANESBILL
Geranium

The quietly lovely, modest-sized plants called cranesbills are members of the genus *Geranium*. But there is another kind of plant also called geranium — the bedding plants that were so wildly popular with American gardeners à generation ago and that are still important to that industry — which actually belong to the genus *Pelargonium*. British gardeners very sensibly call them pelargoniums, eliminating the confusion on their side of the Atlantic. But Americans still persist,

for the most part, in calling both kinds of plants geraniums.

Geranium comes from the Greek word *geranos*, which means "crane." The name describes the seed capsules, which are long, pointed, and shaped something like the beak of a crane. *Pelargonium* is from the Greek *pelargos*, meaning "stork," and also refers to the shape of the seed pods.

Some of the more interestingly named cranesbill species include *Geranium cinereum* ("gray"), which has grayish green leaves; *endressii*, which was named for P. A. C. Endress, who discovered the plant growing wild in the Pyrenees in 1812; and *sanguineum* ("bloody"), which has flowers that are reddish purple in color.

CUPID'S DART
Catananche

At first glance the genus name of this not-terribly-well-known garden flower seems unremarkable. Many sources simply say *Catananche* comes from the Greek name for the plant. But dig a little deeper into its origins and a more interesting story emerges. The Greek name is based on a word meaning, roughly, "compulsion." A rather odd idea, naming a plant compulsion — it sounds more like the name of a modern perfume. But *Catananche* is also the common Greek word for "spell" (as in magic spell), and this plant was used in love potions. The flower's common name is Cupid's dart, and apparently the Greeks believed it could inspire passion just as those heavenly arrows did.

The flower itself does little to suggest its namesake. It has no dart-shaped parts in its structure, and it isn't Valentine pink or red. In fact, the only species that's seen in gardens, *Catananche caerulea*, has blue flowers (*caerulea* means "deep blue").

What's the recipe for a love potion made with Cupid's dart? Alas, the Greeks did not pass down the formula along with the name. Perhaps the heavenly color alone, when presented to the loved one in a large enough bouquet, can easily inspire tender feelings.

DAFFODIL

Narcissus

The fanciful blossoms of the genus *Narcissus*, which includes daffodils as well as the flowers whose common name is also narcissus, have several petals fused into a central cup. A lawn of naturalized daffodils brings to mind a host of yellow-gowned ladies waltzing in the grass, certainly the inspiration for the nursery rhyme about Daffy Down-Dilly who comes to town in her yellow petticoat.

Narcissus was named for a legendary Greek youth whose beauty attracted the attention of a lovely but talkative nymph named Echo who could only repeat what was said to her. The arrogant youth ignored her, and the broken-hearted Echo wasted away until there was nothing left of her but her voice. The gods punished Narcissus by making him fall in love — with his own reflection. Leaning over a pool one day, he became entranced with the lovely creature looking back at him, but as soon as his fingertip touched the water, the face disappeared. Narcissus was so enraptured that he could not tear himself away from the pool and he eventually died there, turning into the flower that bears his name.

While their mythological namesake was impossible to please, the flowers are most amenable, demanding little and never failing to put on a brilliant show in spring.

DAME'S ROCKET

Hesperis

Strolling through a flower garden on a warm summer evening, it sometimes seems that as colors fade in the dying light, scents intensify — during the day the garden is for the eyes to appreciate, but at night a garden is for the nose. The strengthening of floral fragrance at night is no illusion, for many flowers do smell stronger after dark, in order to attract the nocturnal creatures (generally moths) that pollinate them. One of these flowers of the night is the dame's rocket, *Hesperis matronalis.*

Hesperis is from the Greek *hespera*, which means "evening." The species name, *matronalis*, means "of matrons." This name is supposed to have come from an old name for the flower, mother of the evening.

The flowers of dame's rocket are purple or lilac-purple, the color inspiring another nickname, dame's violet. The sweet fragrance is probably the source of yet another appellation, sweet rocket. The "rocket" part of the name seems to come from the fact that the plant is in the mustard family, which includes the salad green arugula, also known as rocket. Perhaps many family members were once called rocket. The tall, sweet-scented dame's rocket is certainly the nocturnal star of the group.

DAYLILY
Hemerocallis

Surely one of the most rewarding of garden flowers, the daylily has had a rather peripatetic history. Daylilies originated in China, where they are used for a number of culinary and medicinal uses. In the sixteenth century they travelled the Silk Road back to Europe with traders and eventually Dutch settlers brought them to New York. The tawny daylily managed to escape cultivation and set up housekeeping all over the eastern part of the United States, where its orange flowers are a familiar summer sight along roadsides. (This plant's species name is *fulva*, and yes, it does mean "tawny.")

Daylilies also were carried west with the pioneers. It is said that when covered wagons were destroyed or abandoned along the western trails, the daylilies took root and grew, and came to be known as ditch lilies.

Though it is not usually known as a food source, the plant is edible. The flower buds can be dipped in batter and fried (the Chinese call them golden needles), and the fleshy roots are said to have a nutty flavor similar to water chestnuts.

The daylily's generic name comes from the Greek words *hemera*, "day," and *kallos*, which means "beauty." Although the plants flower for weeks, each individual blossom lasts but a single day.

DELPHINIUM

Delphinium

Some plants are named for their resemblance to animals. The stately delphinium is one such flower. One of the aristocrats of the English flower border, it bears its lovely blue (or purple or pink or white) blossoms on tall spikes, and with its slender spur, the flower might remind the careful observer of the nose of a bottle-nosed dolphin. It is from this resemblance that the plant received its generic name, which is based on the Greek word for "dolphin," *delphis*.

A closely related flower is the larkspur, whose common name is also based upon the spurred structure of its blossoms. A lark, of course, is a bird, and perhaps the name comes from the "horns" on one type of lark. The best-known larkspur was originally named *Delphinium ajacis* (its botanical name has since been changed to *Consolida ambigua*). *Ajacis* comes from Ajax, one of the legendary heroes of the Trojan War. According to the story, when Achilles was killed by the Trojans, his mother, Thetis, a sea nymph, asked the Greek leaders to give her son's armor to the next best and bravest fighter among their troops. Ajax expected that the armor would be given to him, but it went instead to Ulysses. Ajax was so distraught that he killed himself (which would seem to indicate that he wasn't truly worthy of the prize), and wherever his blood spilled larkspurs grew.

FOXGLOVE
Digitalis

According to one legend, fairies made the blossoms of foxglove and gave them to friendly foxes to wear as gloves so they could sneak into the local henhouse for a chicken dinner without getting caught. In fact, most of the names for these handsome spikes of elongated, bell-shaped blossoms (actually they *are* rather like fingers, too) seem to have something to do with articles of clothing. The genus name comes from the Latin *digitus*, meaning "finger." In France the flower has been called Our Lady's gloves, *les gants de Notre Dame*. In Ireland it has gone by the name fairy's cap.

Foxglove leaves contain a medicinal substance called digitalin, and they have been used to treat heart problems since the eighteenth century. Traditionally the foxglove plant was supposed to be picked with the left hand if it was going to be effective in healing. But if you pick the flowers you are apt to deprive the fairies of their millinery and the foxes of their gloves, so foxglove is undoubtedly best enjoyed in the flower garden. Besides, another name for the plant is deadman's bells, and it can be quite poisonous if the wrong amount is used — so perhaps it's best to refrain yourself from picking the flowers altogether.

IRIS

Iris

This beautiful flower, which comes in so many colors, was named for the Greek goddess of the rainbow. Iris tinted the sky with her rainbow, and traveled over it to carry messages from the gods and goddesses to favored mortals on earth. Iris was also responsible for conveying the souls of women to the Elysian Fields; sorrowing widowers planted the flowers on the graves of their departed wives to honor the rainbow goddess. The iris was a flower of communication; in the flower language of Victorian England, receiving an iris meant that the sender had a special message for you.

Irises are among the oldest known cultivated plants — people have grown them since at least 1000 B.C. A painting found on the wall of King Minos' palace in Crete shows a boy amid a host of blooming irises; the Egyptian pharoah Thutmose III had irises in his palace gardens; the Romans used the iris motif to decorate tombs; and early Muslims planted them in their cemeteries, too. Along with the lily, the iris symbolized the Virgin Mary and the flowers appeared in fifteenth-century Flemish altarpieces and religious paintings.

In imperial Japan, irises were not on the approved list of garden flowers, but inventive gardeners got around the ban by planting them on roofs. One species of iris native to the Far East is still called the "roof iris."

LAVENDER
Lavandula

The fragrant lavender takes both its scientific and common names from the Latin word *lavo*, meaning "to wash." The Romans perfumed their bath water with the leaves and flowers of lavender. It is still a favorite ingredient in bath and cosmetic preparations, scented soaps, bubble bath, colognes, body lotions, herbal bath mixtures, and potpourris and sachets. Sprigs of lavender can be placed among linens folded for storage to give them a fresh scent and in England this practice gave rise to the expression "laid up in lavender."

A charming story in the Christian tradition tells how the lavender plant got its sweet, refreshing fragrance. According to the tale, Mary once hung the infant Jesus' freshly washed clothes to dry on a lavender bush (the plant has a shrubby form in warm climates). When the clothes had dried they smelled clean and fresh, and so did the plant.

In addition to its healing qualities and pleasant scent, lavender also carries with it some unpleasant associations. To the Victorians lavender symbolized distrust, apparently because of an old belief that the asp that killed Cleopatra hid under a lavender bush. Another old superstition holds that if you carry a sprig of lavender you will be able to see ghosts.

LILAC
Syringa

The lilac's common name is derived from the Persian word for "blue," the same as the lovely pastel bluish purple color of its fragrant flowers. Most of our familiar garden lilacs are descendants of the common European species *Syringa vulgaris*, whose species name means "common."

The plant's genus name is rooted in a mythological tale of unrequited love. The word is from the Greek *syrinx*, meaning "pipe," and refers to the plant's hollow stems. A syrinx is not just any kind of pipe—it is the name of the pipe of Pan,

whose haunting sound perfectly reflects its sad origins.

Syrinx, a nymph, was a follower of Diana, the virgin goddess of the hunt, and she had no interest in romance. Syrinx spurned the attentions of all her would-be suitors, including those of Pan, the goat-footed god of shepherds. Not one to take rejection easily, Pan pursued Syrinx through the forest. The nymph ran until she collapsed on the bank of a river, exhausted, with Pan hot on her heels. Her friends the water nymphs came to Syrinx's aid, and when Pan triumphantly went to embrace her, he found himself hugging a clump of reeds instead. His beloved lost to him, Pan cut the reeds into several lengths and made a pipe upon which he played the plaintive melodies of his broken heart.

LUNGWORT
Pulmonaria

The root of this genus name is the Latin *pulmo*, or "lung" (the same word that provides the basis for "pulmonary," the term for anything involving the lungs), and, in fact, the Latin *pulmonaria* means "beneficial to the lungs." In this case, the plant's common name, lungwort, reflects its usage — indicating that the plant was prescribed to treat lung ailments (remember, the suffix "-wort" indicates a plant that had medicinal applications).

The most often grown species of lungwort is *Pulmonaria saccharata*, also known as Bethlehem sage. The species name means "sprinkled with sugar," a quaint way of noting this plant's distinctive white spots on the lower leaves. Some sources mention that the spotted leaves might have put medieval healers in mind of diseased lungs. According to the Doctrine of Signatures, popular in the sixteenth century, treatments for illnesses were found in plants resembling the ailing body part. Since lungwort leaves looked like a person's ailing lungs, they would be used to treat bronchial problems.

Other non-lung-related names for *Pulmonaria* include soldiers-and-sailors, soldier-and-his-wife, and boys-and-girls — all references to the tendency of single plants to bear both pink and blue flowers.

MARIGOLD
Tagetes

Marigold is a shortened form of "Mary's gold" — the richness of the flowers' golden hue was deemed worthy of the Virgin Mary. The flowers that gardeners today know as marigolds, members of the genus *Tagetes*, have a wealth of meanings, symbols, and stories associated with their names. The genus name commemorates an Etruscan deity, Tages, a grandson of Jupiter who first learned the art of divination and taught it to the Etruscans. Tages was believed to have sprung as a boy from a field of newly ploughed earth.

Marigolds, which are native to Mexico, were sacred to the Aztecs. It is said that after the conquest of Cortés the Aztecs regarded the red splotches on the golden blossoms of one type of marigold as a symbol of the Indian blood that was spilled on the gold stolen by the conquistadores. The flower came to symbolize sorrow and pain, and was called *flor de muerte*.

The Spanish conquerors took the golden flower back to Europe along with their spoils. Seeds of two types were taken to Spain by priests returning with Cortés. From Spain one species made its way to Africa, and the other to France. Eventually seeds were taken to England and planted in gardens there, and the flowers became known as African and French marigolds.

MORNING GLORY
I p o m o e a

↳ The name "morning glory" came about because each of these flowers blooms for only a single day. In the English countryside gardeners sometimes referred to the plant as "life of man," because its flowering imitated the stages of a human life: the flowers are in bud in their morning childhood, fully open at midday, and wilting in their old age in the evening. Other nicknames for the plant include old man's nightcap ("old man" was a name for the devil), for the long, slender throats of the flower could resemble a nightcap in shape;

and devil's guts, a reference to the plant's curled tendrils.

There are two conflicting descriptions of the origin of the genus name, *Ipomoea*. The name is derived from the Greek words *ips* and *homios*. Some sources say *ips* means "a worm," and others say it means "bindweed"; the word *homios* means "resembling." So *Ipomoea* means either "resembling a worm," an apparent reference to the spiralling tendrils by which it climbs, or "resembling bindweed," which it certainly does. Bindweed, for those lucky gardeners who have never encountered it, is a wild plant that grows like crazy and looks much like the cultivated morning glory. Both belong to the family Convolvulaceae, the name of which is derived from the Latin word *convolvere*, which means "to entwine."

PHEASANT'S EYE
Adonis

🖎 *Adonis annua* got its nickname because its red flowers have a dark central spot, like the eye of a pheasant.

The genus name has a more complicated story. In classical mythology, Venus beheld the handsome youth Adonis after she had been accidentally pricked by one of Cupid's arrows. Smitten with Adonis' looks, Venus left Olympus to follow him wherever he went. One of his favorite pastimes was hunting, and Venus, fearing for the safety of her beloved, warned him to be careful of dangerous animals. Adonis, being nobly born, paid little attention to the goddess's warnings. One day he spotted a wild boar in the forest and threw his spear at the beast, striking it in the side. But the boar pulled out the weapon with its teeth and charged at Adonis, fatally goring him with its long tusks.

Venus found the dying Adonis in the woods and in her grief declared that his blood would be transformed into flowers whose bloom would each year commemorate her sorrow and his death. Flowers sprang up at once from the blood-soaked ground — flowers as red as the boy's blood.

PINK

Dianthus

The garden pinks of the genus *Dianthus* arrived at their shared common name in a most obvious way: the flowers came in many shades of pink, rose, and red. But what of their individual names? One species is called the grass pink, an allusion to the narrow, bladelike leaves they all share. Another species, the maiden pink, is a charming little plant with flowers the color of a young girl's blush. Allwood pinks were named for their breeders, the Allwood brothers. But the evocative names of the cheddar pink and the sweet William remain a cause for speculation.

If there were an award for best fragrance in a flower, it should be given to the garden pinks. Many members of the clan possess a spicy, clovelike aroma that is both sweet and exhilarating.

And as if an unparalleled perfume weren't enough, the flowers are pretty, too. From the dainty, fringed-petalled maiden pinks to the rich, rose-and-wine-colored, gorgeously striped sweet William, *Dianthus* flowers are stunners. They have, in short, everything it takes to make a perfect flower.

The Greeks must have been equally enthusiastic about *Dianthus*. Their name for them comes from *di*, "of Zeus," and *anthos*, "a flower." Literally "the flower of Zeus," the name is interpreted to mean "divine flower," which surely they are.

POT MARIGOLD
Calendula

In 1818, John Keats immortalized the humble pot marigold in these lines from "I Stood Tiptoe Upon a Little Hill":

Open fresh your round of starry folds

Ye ardent marigolds!

The marigold of the Romantics and other poets was not the same flower most of us think of today as the marigold. It was instead the calendula. The plant eventually acquired its nickname of pot marigold because it was so frequently grown in containers, kitchen gardens, and flower gardens. It has also been called summer's bride or husbandman's dial, a reference to the way the flowers turn their heads to follow the sun across the sky each day.

The generic name is derived from the Latin *calendae*, meaning "month," or "the first day of the month," when the plant was supposedly always in bloom. The name describes the plant's long blooming period; although it doesn't quite bloom year-round, it does flower for months at a time.

The best-known species is *Calendula officinalis*. The name *officinalis* designates a plant that once had medicinal uses, and the lovely garden flower has enjoyed a long history as an herbal remedy for a multitude of ills.

PRIMROSE
Primula

The primrose is a favorite spring flower in English gardens. Its name comes from the Latin *primus*, or "first." Although primroses are not really among the first flowers to bloom in spring, perhaps the name means "first rose," and primroses certainly bloom before roses. The Victorians assigned to primroses a connotation of early youth. In the late nineteenth century, the date of Benjamin Disraeli's death, April 19, was named Primrose Day in England to honor the statesman whose favorite flower it was.

The plant carries its flowers in a cluster, which has inspired several nicknames comparing the blossoms to a bunch of keys: Our Lady's keys, for example, little keys to heaven, and St. Peter's keys. A belief sprang up that the flowers could unlock treasure chests. It is said that St. Peter, who admits deserving souls to heaven, found out that some souls of questionable integrity were trying to sneak into heaven through the back door instead of the Pearly Gates. Poor St. Peter was so shaken by the news that he dropped the keys, which fell to earth and turned into primroses.

As a flower of English fields and meadows, primroses are rumored to offer shelter for fairies when the rain falls. Thus, they have been called fairy flower, fairy basin, and fairy cup.

ST. JOHN'S-WORT
Hypericum

There are a number of meanings assigned to the name *Hypericum*. According to one story the plant was named for Hyperion, the Greek Titan who was the father of Helios, the sun. In Norse mythology, too, the plant was associated with the sun; it was dedicated to Baldur, the sun god. And, in pre-Christian Europe the plant was burned on Midsummer's Eve (the summer solstice) to honor the sun and maintain the good will of benevolent spirits. People living on the Isle of Wight believed that stepping on a *Hypericum* plant at night summoned a ghostly horse that would carry them off on a wild, night-long ride.

The early Christians, anxious to put a stop to the old pagan rituals and superstitions, named the plant St. John's-wort, in honor of John the Baptist, whose saint's day fell near Midsummer's Eve. The ancient solstice festival became the Feast of St. John on June 24. It was said that if you picked St. John's-wort on St. John's eve, you would be able to see where witches were holding their midsummer celebrations.

The suffix "-wort" in a plant's common name indicates that it was once used in healing, and St. John's-wort is no exception. Medieval monks grew it in their monastery gardens and used it to heal wounds and treat sore throats.

SNAPDRAGON

Antirrhinum

🌿 Any child whose mother grew snapdragons in her flower beds knows that when you pick a snapdragon and pinch it at the base you can make the flower's two halves open and close, like the jaws of an animal. Why is it a dragon whose jaws are snapping shut? No one knows for sure, but one old tradition associates it with the legend of St. George and the dragon. Those enormous fire-breathing serpents of European mythology, awesome and terrible, stalk across the pages of fairy tales amassing hoards of gold and jewels in their cavernous

lairs and threatening fair maidens (who must be time and again rescued by valiant knights in shining armor). The knights of King Arthur's Round Table had dragons to fight when they weren't busy chasing the Saxons from the shores of Britain. That a snapdragon flower represents a dragon was probably a tale told to amuse a child sometime long ago.

In the case of the snapdragon, the botanical and common names are closely related, both describing the structure of the flower. The botanical name comes from two Greek words: *anti*, which means "like," and *rhis*, meaning "snout." Indeed, the flowers do remind one of an animal's snout — they are tubular in form and have two lips that come together. They are the least frightening dragons you will ever encounter.

SUNFLOWER

Helianthus and *Heliopsis*

Several kinds of glowing golden sunflowers belong to these two genera. It is obvious that both names are built from the same word — *helios*, Greek for "sun." *Helianthus* adds *anthos*, "flower," so its name is literally sunflower. *Heliopsis* combines *helios* with *-opsis*, which indicates resemblance, and the name thus means "resembling the sun." When you consider the disc-shaped flowers with their sunny yellow petals (appropriately enough, those petallike structures are not true petals, but are correctly called rays), their naming seems fitting indeed.

Sunflowers are native to the Americas, and they have been an important part of the life of a variety of American cultures. In Peru the Incas worshipped the sunflower as a symbol of the sun. The sunflower was also a source of food for Indians in various parts of South America.

In the United States, pioneer families on the Great Plains depended on sunflowers for food, cooking oil, animal fodder, and other necessities. They planted sunflowers close to their houses, thinking that the flowers would offer protection against malaria.

Like its celestial namesake, the sunflower has been, and continues to be, a source of life for people on earth.

YARROW
Achillea

Yarrow has a long history as a healing plant. The name may be derived from an old Anglo-Saxon word, *gearwe*, which meant "ready to heal." The plant has also been called staunchgrass, woundwort, bloodwort, and nosebleed.

The genus name of *Achillea*, a rather modest plant in its wild form, commemorates one of the most celebrated heroes of Greek mythology, Achilles.

As legend had it, Achilles was the son of a sea nymph, Thetis, and he came to glory on the battlefields of the Trojan

War. This war, you may recall, was fought because Paris, the son of the King of Troy, kidnapped Helen, who was the wife of King Menelaus of Sparta. Achilles was the bravest, most powerful warrior on the Greek side. He seemed to be invincible, a result of his mother having dipped him, as a baby, in magic waters that protected him from injury in battle. His only vulnerable spot was his heel, by which Thetis held the baby while dipping him (hence the origin of the "Achilles heel").

It was said that the mighty Achilles used his namesake plant to stop the bleeding and heal the wounds of his soldiers. And that is how herbalists have used it ever since. The flowers hold their color well when dried, and make a lovely addition to dried arrangements.

LIST OF
ILLUSTRATIONS